THE TINAJA TONIGHT

Aimée M. Bissonette

illustrated by
Syd Weiler

Albert Whitman & Company
Chicago, Illinois

Hot wind.
Cracked earth.
Dust and rock.
Scorching sun.

Can anything live in this stark, empty world?
Whose feet pound this hard, packed dirt?
Who can make a meal of sagebrush, agave, and prickly pear?

There is little moisture in desert air, so temperatures change a lot from day to night. Daytime temperatures average 100°F, while nighttime temperatures can drop to below freezing.

Plants store water.
Animals get their
water from food, and
avoid activity during
the hot day.

Desert plants
and animals live
with extreme
temperatures and
a lack of water.

You do not see them, but they are there—
    under bushes,
    beneath rock ledges,
    crouching in shallow dens, bellies pressed to the earth.

They are there, and they are waiting.
Waiting for the sun to set.
Waiting for the air to cool.
Waiting for darkness, when at last it will be time...
    to scamper, hearts racing, across slick rock,
    to scuttle down washes of shifting, loose stone,
    to slip through the shadows of a red sandstone cliff,
    to drink the saving water of the tinaja.

Desert animals come
to the tinaja at night
because the desert is too
hot during the day for
them to come out.

A tinaja is a pool formed by a natural hollow in the rock where rainwater or melting snow collects. Tinajas hold water for different lengths of time before it evaporates. They're an important source of desert water.

When fast-flowing water cuts into rock on a creek bed, a wash forms—a gully with rushing rainwater.

At the tinaja, everyone drinks.

A family of quail, clucking and crowing. They gather at dusk but keep their eyes on the sky. Falcons and hawks are a quail's biggest worry. But other predators lurk in the rocks and the brush.

What's that sound? What's that snuffling?
The quail take off running.

If only they knew not to worry. It's just...

Desert quail can fly only short distances,
but they run fast—up to 22 mph.

They nest 1–2 feet above ground, near
prickly pear cacti, spiny trees and shrubs
of mesquite, and acacia shrubs and trees,
where their chicks can hide.

snorting, smelly javelina—ten or twenty at a time.
They splash and roll in the pool's cooling water.
But they are watchful—always watchful. Do they
sense others coming? If so, off they trot.
Even if it's only…

Javelina are mostly vegetarian, eating agave and prickly pear, but they'll also eat lizards, rodents, and dead birds.

Javelina roam in herds of up to twenty to protect themselves from mountain lions, bobcats, coyotes, and owls.

jackrabbits, whose long ears help keep them cool during the day. They also use their ears to listen for danger. A twig snaps. The rabbits tremble. Do they run? Do they hide? No need to do either. It's...

If jackrabbits get too hot, they lose excess heat through their big ears. They don't sweat.

They watch for danger with large eyes that allow them to see almost 360 degrees.

They escape from predators with long, strong hind legs that help them run up to 35 mph, and leap more than 15 feet.

mule deer, who have slipped through the trees. Nervous. Uneasy. They scan the woods as they drink. They lift their heads. What's that smell? Who is coming? They startle and bolt when...

Mule deer are named for
their large ears, that look
like mules' ears.

Excellent hearing and
eyesight help warn mule
deer of danger.

They hide among the desert
plants, shrubs, and grasses
that they also eat.

a family of coyotes ambles down for a drink. Adults and young pups, they are panting and parched. They scare off other animals and take over the tinaja. But even they do not linger. Even coyotes can be prey.

Coyotes burrow under trees, bushes, ledges, or outcroppings to sleep.

They "sing" to communicate with one another, keeping track of family members.

Recently, coyotes have moved to cities and suburbs where food is plentiful.

A mountain lion approaches. Silent and sleek. Large front paws, heavy claws; it has nothing to fear. It circles the tinaja with a slow sort of swagger. The mountain lion is king of the life-giving pool.

Mountain lions, or cougars, pumas, or panthers,
are at the top of the desert food chain.
They prey on deer, sheep, cattle, and horses.
They also hunt rodents and grouse.

They are skilled, and wait patiently
to ambush their prey.

Mountain lions are suited to the desert because
they can go for long periods without water.

All night, back and forth, the
visitors exchange places.
    Ringtails,
    desert foxes,
    screech owls,
    bats.

Shy ringtail cats are
part of the raccoon
family, with big eyes,
long striped tails,
sharp claws, and
pointed faces.

Bats eat by scooping insects with their tail membranes or catching them in their open mouths as they fly.

Desert, or kit, foxes weigh only 4–6 pounds and are from 17–21 inches long— about the size of a house cat.

Like jackrabbits, desert foxes have large ears that help reduce body heat.

They watch, and they drink.
Some wash dusty feathers.

Tonight there is water for all
to share...

Screech owls' ear openings are on
the sides of their heads.

These owls eat mice, shrews,
lizards, flying insects—even the
occasional scorpion.

Mojave rattlesnakes
have keen senses of
taste and smell that
help them detect water
over great distances.

They do well in dry climates
because their bodies are
covered in watertight scales
and they drink available
water whenever they can.

except for the smallest, who would not dare!

Kangaroo rats and pocket mice are burrowing rodents with fur-lined pouches in their cheeks to carry seeds. They are prey for rattlesnakes.

Day breaks. The sun rises.
Dust devils swirl.
Can anything live in this stark, empty world?

At night, without the sun to heat the land, and with little moisture in the air, the heat of the day escapes quickly. The daily temperature can change more than 60ºF from day to night.

In the winter, the temperature at night can drop below freezing, but that dry desert air can let the day get hot very quickly—sometimes reaching over 120ºF.

You know they are there.
You know they are waiting.
You know they'll be back at the tinaja tonight.

Even though water of the tinaja is
available during the day, the temperatures
are too hot for the animals to wander
out. Instead, they hunker down and wait
for the cool of the night.

Javelina snort and sleep beneath mesquite trees.

Jackrabbits rest in the shade of grass or bushes.

Mountain lions seek out caves.

Coyotes return to their dens in the canyons and washes.

Author's Note

Tinajas are desert water holes—natural depressions eroded into the bedrock by weather and water. They are found in the hottest and driest parts of North America and range in size from tiny potholes to large pools. Tinajas are not fed by active streams or springs. They fill with runoff from storms or melting snows in much the same way water from a roof fills a rain barrel.

Some tinajas hold water all year; some, for only a few days or weeks following a rainstorm. Rain is unreliable in the desert, and, over time, much of the water of the tinaja evaporates, or changes from a liquid to a vapor and goes into the air. During the hottest months, desert animals may visit a tinaja one night, only to find it dried up when they return in a few days.

For thousands of years, tinajas have been a vital source of water for animals in the desert Southwest. They also have provided much-needed water for human travelers. In New Mexico's El Morro National Monument, for instance, there is a rare permanent tinaja that has served as an important oasis for travelers for centuries, as is shown by the drawings, signatures, and messages that have been carved in the surrounding rocks by ancestral Puebloans, Spanish conquistadors, and American settlers.

Tinaja is a Spanish word meaning "earthen jar." Tinajas go by other names, too, though. They are sometimes called *huecos*, which means "hollow" in Spanish. They are also referred to as kiss tanks, a name that comes from the eager way the animals of the desert put their dry lips and thirsty mouths to the water to drink.

Resources

activities

Brown, Cynthia Light. *Geology of the Desert Southwest—Investigate How the Earth Was Formed.* White River Junction, VT: Nomad, 2011.

Kavanagh, James R. and Raymond Leung. *Southwest Desert Wildlife Nature Activity Book.* Dunedin, FL: Waterford, 2011.

Krebbs, Karen and Phil Juliana. *Desert Life of the Southwest Activity Book.* Cambridge, MN: Adventure Publications, 2017.

books for children

Arnosky, Jim. *Watching Desert Wildlife.* Washington, DC: National Geographic, 2002.

Laney, Nancy K. *Desert Waters: From Ancient Aquifers to Modern Demands.* Tucson, AZ: Arizona-Sonora Desert Museum, 1998.

Patkau, Karen. *Who Needs a Desert?* Toronto: Tundra, 2014.

Sandstrom, Lee Ann and Karen Shragg. *Nature's Yucky! 2: The Desert Southwest.* Missoula, MT: Mountain Press, 2007.

With love to Bryan, Maureen, and Aliza—
my favorite javelina hunting, red rock hiking buddies!—AMB

Library of Congress Cataloging-in-Publication data is on file with the publisher.
Text copyright © 2020 Aimée M. Bissonette
Illustrations copyright © 2020 by Albert Whitman & Company
Illustrations by Syd Weiler
First published in the United States of America in 2020 by Albert Whitman & Company

ISBN 978-0-8075-7949-7 (hardcover)
ISBN 978-0-8075-7950-3 (ebook)

Printed in China

10 9 8 7 6 5 4 3 2 1 WKT 24 23 22 21 20

Design by Rick DeMonico

For more information about Albert Whitman & Company,
visit our website at www.albertwhitman.com